CRÊPES
AND
QUICHES

mjf
media

Graphic Design Zapp (inside pages) and Cyclone Design
Communications (cover)
Photography Marc Bruneau
Tableware courtesy of Stokes and Hutschenreuter

©2008 Tormont Publications Inc.
This edition printed exclusively for MJF Media.

Canadä
We acknowledge the financial support of the Government of
Canada through the Book Publishing Industry Development
Program (BPIDP) for our publishing activities.

Legal deposit—Bibliothèque et Archives nationales du
Québec, 2008

ISBN 978-2-7641-2284-6 (previously published in hardcover
format by Brimar Publishing, ISBN 2-89433-151-7)

Printed in China

CRÊPES
AND
QUICHES

At first glance, crêpes and quiches
do not seem to have much in common.
But both of them rely on simple
and easy-to-find ingredients
– flour, eggs and milk –
to produce fabulous results
that will make you look like a gourmet cook.

And yet the techniques for making
both quiches and crêpes are extremely easy.
This cookbook will show you the simple
step-by-step procedures for turning out
flaky quiche pastry and crêpes that are light
as a feather.

And the fillings are even easier!
You'll soon discover how simple it is
to transform a few ounces of meat or
a package of spinach or mushrooms into
a satisfying and elegant main course.
Not to mention a variety of ideas for
sophisticated starters and exciting desserts.

This will soon become your favorite cookbook
for those moments when you want to make
something a little special for family or friends.

Basic Quiche Dough
(yield: 1 – 9-in {23-cm} quiche)

2 cups	all-purpose flour	500 mL
½ tsp	salt	2 mL
7 oz	chilled butter	200 g
⅓ cup	ice water	75 mL

1 Sift flour and salt into bowl.

2 Cut butter into small pieces. Incorporate to flour using pastry blender.

3 When butter is coated with flour, add water and mix quickly to form ball. If necessary add a little more water to obtain desired consistency.

4 Turn dough out onto floured work surface and knead several minutes. Shape into ball, wrap in waxed paper and refrigerate 1 hour.

5 Bring to room temperature before rolling.

Extra Rich Quiche Dough
(yield: 1 – 9-in {23-cm} quiche)

1 ½ cups	all-purpose flour	375 mL
½ tsp	salt	2 mL
6 tbsp	chilled butter	90 mL
2 tbsp	chilled shortening	30 mL
5 tbsp	ice water	75 mL

1 Sift flour and salt into bowl.

2 Cut butter and shortening into small pieces. Incorporate to flour using pastry blender.

3 When fat is coated with flour, add water and mix quickly to form ball. If dough does not adhere well, turn out onto floured work surface and knead several minutes.

4 Shape into ball, wrap in waxed paper and refrigerate 1 hour.

5 Bring to room temperature before rolling.

Blind Baking Quiche Dough

1 The quiche recipes in this book use a 9-in (23-cm) round mold. Choose a fluted quiche pan with removable bottom. For variety, a 9-in (23-cm) square mold or a 9 x 13-in (23 x 23-cm) rectangular mold may also be used.

2 Roll out dough on floured work surface to an even ⅛ in (3 mm) thickness.

3 Line mold, pressing dough snug against bottom corners. Using rolling pin, cut off excess dough from rim.

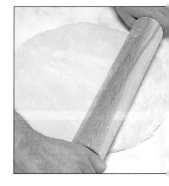

4 Line dough with waxed or parchment paper. Fill with baking weights or dried beans. Precook 12 minutes in oven preheated at 400°F (200°C).

5 Remove paper and weights from dough. Prick bottom of dough with fork and let stand at least 5 minutes before filling. Follow directions in recipe for baking.

6 When quiche is done, let stand several minutes before slicing.

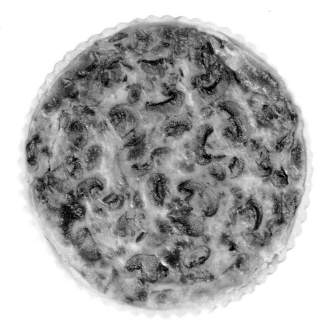

Swiss Mushroom Quiche
(4 servings)

I	quiche shell	I
2 tbsp	butter	30 mL
I	dry shallot, peeled and chopped	I
½ lb	fresh mushrooms, cleaned and sliced	225 g
3 tbsp	flour	45 mL
I cup	milk, heated	250 mL
4 tbsp	heavy cream	60 mL
2	large eggs, beaten	2
I cup	grated Emmenthal cheese	250 mL
	salt and freshly ground pepper	
	pinch of nutmeg	

Preheat oven to 400°F (200°C).

1 Line dough with waxed or parchment paper. Fill with baking weights or dried beans. Precook 12 minutes in oven.

2 Remove paper and weights from dough. Prick bottom of dough with fork and set aside.

3 Reduce oven temperature to 375°F (190°C).

4 Heat butter in frying pan over medium heat. Add shallot and mushrooms; season well. Cook 5 minutes over high heat.

5 Sprinkle in flour and mix well. Pour in milk, mix and add cream. Season well and continue cooking 4 minutes.

6 Remove pan from heat and set mixture aside to cool. When tepid, mix in eggs. Add cheese, pinch of nutmeg and mix again.

7 Transfer mixture to quiche shell. Bake 20 to 25 minutes in oven.

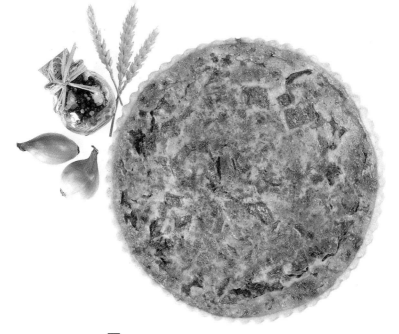

Fresh Tomato Quiche with Gruyère
(4 servings)

2 tbsp	olive oil	30 mL
2	dry shallots, peeled and chopped	2
3	tomatoes, peeled, seeded and coarsely chopped	3
3 tbsp	chopped fresh basil	45 mL
1¼ cups	grated Gruyère cheese	300 mL
2 tbsp	grated Parmesan cheese	30 mL
3	large eggs	3
1	large egg yolk	1
1 cup	heavy cream	250 mL
	salt and pepper	
	paprika to taste	
	precooked quiche shell	

Preheat oven to 375°F (190°C).

1 Heat oil in frying pan over medium heat. Add shallots, tomatoes and basil. Season well and cook 8 minutes over medium heat. Remove pan from heat and set aside.

2 When cooled, transfer tomatoes to quiche shell. Add both cheeses and season well. Add paprika to taste.

3 Mix all eggs and cream together; season well. Pour over cheese and bake quiche 25 to 30 minutes in oven.

Swiss Tuna and Tomato Quiche
(4 servings)

I tbsp	olive oil	15 mL
2	dry shallots, peeled and chopped	2
2	tomatoes, peeled, seeded and chopped	2
I tbsp	chopped fresh parsley	15 mL
2 tbsp	butter	30 mL
2 tbsp	flour	30 mL
I cup	milk, heated	250 mL
3	large eggs, beaten	3
¾ cup	grated Swiss cheese	175 mL
7 oz	can tuna, drained and flaked	198 g
	salt and pepper	
	paprika to taste	
	precooked quiche shell	

Preheat oven to 375°F (190°C).

1 Heat oil in frying pan over medium heat. Add shallots and tomatoes; season well. Increase heat to high and cook 8 minutes. Stir in parsley, remove pan from heat and set aside to cool.

2 Heat butter in saucepan over medium heat. Sprinkle in flour and mix well. Add milk and whisk to incorporate. Season, add paprika and cook sauce 6 minutes over low heat. Remove pan from heat.

3 When white sauce is cool, whisk in beaten eggs and cheese. Correct seasoning.

4 Spread tuna over bottom of quiche shell. Add tomatoes, then white egg sauce. Bake 20 to 30 minutes in oven.

Classic Onion and Cheese Quiche
(4 servings)

2 tbsp	butter	30 mL
5	onions, peeled and thinly sliced	5
1 tsp	granulated sugar	5 mL
1 tbsp	chopped fresh tarragon	15 mL
1 tbsp	chopped fresh parsley	15 mL
1 cup	grated Emmenthal cheese	250 mL
3	large eggs	3
1	large egg yolk	1
1 cup	light cream	250 mL
	salt and pepper	
	precooked quiche shell	
	pinch of cayenne pepper and nutmeg	

Preheat oven to 375°F (190°C).

1 Heat butter in sauté pan over medium heat. Add onions, season well and cook 25 minutes over low heat. Onions must brown, but not burn. Stir 6 times during cooking.

2 Sprinkle in sugar and all seasonings; mix well. Continue cooking 4 to 5 minutes, stirring once.

3 Transfer onions to quiche shell. Top with cheese.

4 Mix all eggs and cream together; season well. Pour over cheese and bake quiche 25 to 30 minutes in oven.

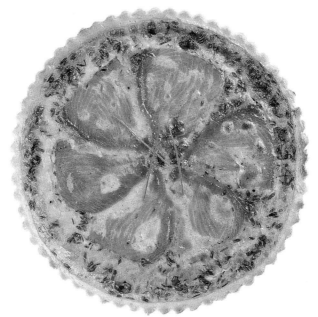

Elegant Smoked Salmon Quiche
(4 servings)

6	slices smoked salmon	6
½ cup	grated Emmenthal cheese	125 mL
½ cup	grated Gruyère cheese	125 mL
1 tbsp	chopped fresh basil	15 mL
1 tbsp	chopped fresh chives	15 mL
3	large eggs	3
1	large egg yolk	1
1 cup	heavy cream	250 mL
	precooked quiche shell	
	salt and freshly ground pepper	
	cayenne pepper to taste	

Preheat oven to 375°F (190°C).

1 Fold each slice of salmon in half and arrange in quiche shell. Top with both cheese and herbs; season with pepper.

2 Mix all eggs and cream together; season well. Add cayenne pepper to taste. Pour over cheese and bake quiche 25 to 30 minutes in oven.

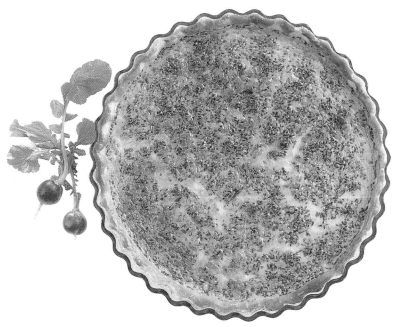

Quiche Lorraine
(4 servings)

6	slices crisp-cooked bacon, chopped	6
½ cup	grated Parmesan cheese	125 mL
⅓ lb	Emmenthal cheese, diced	150 g
3	large eggs	3
1	large egg yolk	1
1 cup	light cream	250 mL
2 tbsp	chopped fresh chives	30 mL
1 tbsp	chopped fresh basil	15 mL
	precooked quiche shell	
	salt and freshly ground pepper	

Preheat oven to 375°F (190°C).

1 Spread chopped bacon over bottom of quiche shell. Sprinkle with Parmesan cheese and add diced Emmenthal. Season generously.

2 Mix all eggs and cream together; season well. Add fresh herbs and mix again. Pour over cheese and bake quiche 25 to 30 minutes in oven.

Garlicky Tomato and Sausage Quiche Pie
(4 servings)

1	quiche shell	1
2 tbsp	butter	30 mL
3	onions, peeled and thinly sliced	3
½ lb	fresh mushrooms, cleaned and sliced	225 g
2	garlic cloves, peeled, crushed and chopped	2
1 tbsp	olive oil	15 mL
2	large sausages, sliced ¼ in (5 mm) thick	2
1 cup	grated Gruyère cheese	250 mL
4	large tomatoes, sliced ⅓ in (8 mm) thick	4
1 tsp	olive oil	5 mL
	salt and freshly ground pepper	

Preheat oven to 400°F (200°C).

1 Line dough with waxed or parchment paper. Fill with baking weights or dried beans. Precook 15 minutes in oven.

2 Remove paper and weights from dough. Prick bottom of dough with fork and set aside.

3 Reduce oven temperature to 375°F (190°C).

4 Heat butter in frying pan over medium heat. Add onions, season well and cook 14 minutes over low heat.

5 Stir in mushrooms and garlic. Continue cooking 5 minutes. Transfer contents of pan to bowl and set aside.

6 Return pan to heat and add 1 tbsp (15 mL) oil. When hot, add sausages and cook 4 minutes. Season with pepper.

7 Fill quiche shell with layer of onions, cheese, sausages and tomatoes. Drizzle remaining olive oil over tomatoes.

8 Bake 18 to 20 minutes in oven.

Heat butter in frying pan over medium heat. Add onions, season well and cook 14 minutes over low heat.

Stir in mushrooms and garlic. Continue cooking 5 minutes. Transfer contents of pan to bowl and set aside.

Return pan to heat and add 1 tbsp (15 mL) oil. When hot, add sausages and cook 4 minutes.

Fill quiche shell with layer of onions and cheese.

Add layer of sausages and layer of tomatoes.

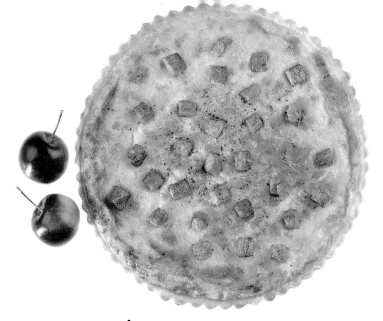

Apple and Bacon Quiche
(4 servings)

2 tbsp	butter	30 mL
5	slices back bacon, diced	5
3	apples, cored, peeled and diced	3
1 cup	grated Swiss cheese	250 mL
3	large eggs	3
1	large egg yolk	1
1 cup	heavy cream	250 mL
	salt and pepper	
	pinch of nutmeg and paprika	
	precooked quiche shell	

Preheat oven to 375°F (190°C).

1 Heat butter in frying pan over medium heat. Add bacon and cook 3 minutes over high heat. Add apples and continue cooking 5 minutes.

2 Let cool, then transfer mixture to quiche shell. Top with cheese and season with salt, pepper, nutmeg and paprika.

3 Mix all eggs and cream together; season well. Pour over cheese and bake quiche 25 to 30 minutes in oven.

Fresh Green Bean Quiche with Chèvre
(4 servings)

1 lb	fresh green beans, pared	450 g
1 tbsp	butter	15 mL
2	dry shallots, peeled and chopped	2
3	large eggs	3
1	large egg yolk	1
1 cup	heavy cream	250 mL
3 oz	goat cheese, in pieces	90 g
	precooked quiche shell	
	salt and pepper	

Preheat oven to 375°F (190°C).

1 Cook beans 10 minutes in salted, boiling water. Drain well and set aside.

2 Heat butter in frying pan over medium heat. Add shallots and green beans; cook 3 minutes.

3 Transfer cooked beans to quiche shell and season well.

4 Mix all eggs, cream and goat cheese together; season well. Pour over beans and bake quiche 25 to 30 minutes in oven.

Swiss-Style Quiche
(4 servings)

2 tbsp	butter	30 mL
2 tbsp	flour	30 mL
1½ cups	milk, heated	375 mL
1	small onion, peeled and studded with clove	1
¼ cup	heavy cream	50 mL
3	large eggs	3
1 cup	grated Gruyère cheese	250 mL
	salt and pepper	
	pinch of nutmeg	
	precooked quiche shell	

Preheat oven to 375°F (190°C).

1 Heat butter in saucepan over medium heat. Sprinkle in flour and mix well. Pour in milk and whisk to incorporate. Season and add studded onion. Cook sauce 8 minutes over low heat, stirring occasionally.

2 Add heavy cream and continue cooking 3 minutes. Transfer contents of pan to bowl and set aside to cool. Discard onion.

3 Add eggs to sauce and mix well. Stir in cheese, season generously and add pinch of nutmeg.

4 Pour mixture into quiche shell and bake 30 minutes in oven or until nicely browned.

Spicy Salami Quiche with Double Cheese
(4 servings)

10	slices spicy Italian salami, in julienne	10
2 tbsp	chopped fresh parsley	30 mL
1 cup	grated Gruyère cheese	250 mL
¼ cup	grated Parmesan cheese	50 mL
3	large eggs	3
1	large egg yolk	1
1 cup	light cream	250 mL
	precooked quiche shell	
	salt and freshly ground pepper	

Preheat oven to 375°F (190°C).

1 Spread strips of salami over bottom of quiche shell. Sprinkle with parsley and top with both cheeses.

2 Mix all eggs with cream; season well. Pour over cheese and bake quiche 25 to 30 minutes in oven.

Madeira Crab and Shrimp Quiche
(4 servings)

1 tbsp	butter	15 mL
2	dry shallots, peeled and chopped	2
½ lb	fresh crabmeat	225 g
4	fresh shrimp, peeled, deveined and diced	4
1 tbsp	chopped fresh basil	15 mL
1 tbsp	chopped fresh parsley	15 mL
2 tbsp	Madeira wine	30 mL
1 cup	grated Gruyère cheese	250 mL
3	large eggs	3
1	large egg yolk	1
1 cup	heavy cream	250 mL
	salt and pepper	
	pinch of cayenne pepper and nutmeg	
	precooked quiche shell	

1 Heat butter in frying pan over high heat. Add shallots, crabmeat and shrimp. Season well and cook 2 minutes.

2 Add herbs and wine. Continue cooking 1 minute over high heat.

3 Transfer mixture to quiche shell and spread evenly. Top with cheese and season with cayenne pepper and nutmeg.

4 Mix all eggs and cream together; season well. Pour over cheese and bake quiche 25 to 30 minutes in oven.

Regal Lobster Quiche
(4 servings)

1 tbsp	butter	15 mL
1½ cups	cubed cooked lobster meat	375 mL
1	dry shallot, peeled and chopped	1
1 tbsp	chopped fresh parsley	15 mL
1½ cups	grated Gruyère cheese	375 mL
2	large eggs	2
1	large egg yolk	1
1 cup	heavy cream	250 mL
	salt and pepper	
	precooked quiche shell	
	cayenne pepper to taste	

Preheat oven to 375°F (190°C).

1 Heat butter in frying pan over medium heat. Add lobster, shallot and parsley. Season and cook 2 minutes.

2 Let cool, then transfer mixture to quiche shell. Add cheese and season well. Sprinkle with cayenne pepper to taste.

3 Mix all eggs and cream together; season well. Pour over cheese and bake quiche 25 to 30 minutes in oven.

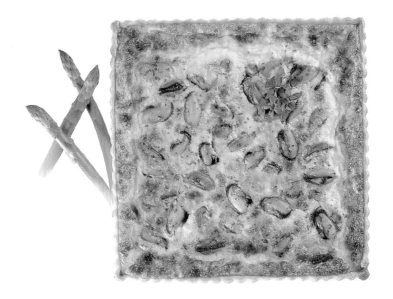

Mussel Quiche with Gruyère
(4 servings)

2 lb	fresh mussels, bearded and scrubbed	900 g
4 tbsp	butter	60 mL
2 tbsp	chopped fresh parsley	30 mL
2	dry shallots, peeled and chopped	2
½ cup	dry white wine	125 mL
2 tbsp	flour	30 mL
½ cup	heavy cream	125 mL
1½ cups	grated Gruyère cheese	375 mL
	sprig of fresh thyme	
	salt and freshly ground pepper	
	precooked quiche shell	

Preheat oven to 425°F (220°C).

1 Place mussels, half of butter and parsley, shallots, thyme sprig and wine in pot. Season with pepper.

2 Cover and bring to boil. Cook mussels over low heat until shells open, about 5 minutes. Stir once during cooking.

3 Remove mussels from pot, discarding any unopened shells. Detach mussels from shells and set aside. Pass cooking liquid through sieve lined with cheesecloth into small saucepan. Cook liquid 3 minutes over high heat to yield 1 cup (250 mL). Set aside.

4 Heat remaining butter in separate saucepan over medium heat. Sprinkle in flour and mix well. Cook 30 seconds.

5 Incorporate reduced cooking liquid and heavy cream. Mix well and season generously. Stir in remaining parsley.

6 Spread cheese over bottom of quiche shell. Add mussels and pour in sauce. Bake 12 minutes.

Place mussels, half of butter and parsley, shallots, wine and thyme sprig in pot. Cook mussels over low heat until shells open, about 5 minutes.

Pass cooking liquid through sieve lined with cheesecloth into small saucepan.

Heat remaining butter in separate saucepan over medium heat. Sprinkle in flour and mix well. Cook 30 seconds.

Incorporate reduced cooking liquid and heavy cream. Mix well and season generously.

Spread cheese over bottom of quiche shell. Add mussels and pour in sauce.

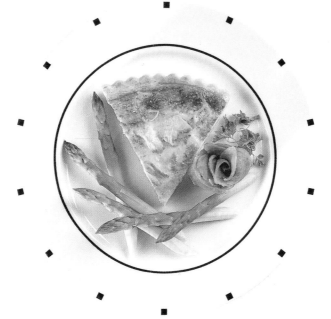

Salmon and Hard-Boiled Egg Quiche
(4 servings)

8 oz	cooked salmon, flaked	225 g
2	hard-boiled eggs, sliced	2
2	large eggs	2
1	large egg yolk	1
1 cup	light cream	250 mL
½ cup	grated Gruyère cheese	125 mL
	precooked quiche shell	
	salt and freshly ground pepper	
	paprika to taste	

Preheat oven to 375°F (190°C).

1 Spread flaked salmon and sliced hard-boiled eggs over bottom of quiche shell. Season and sprinkle with paprika.

2 Mix all eggs and cream together; season well.

3 Pour into quiche shell and add cheese. Bake quiche 25 to 30 minutes in oven.

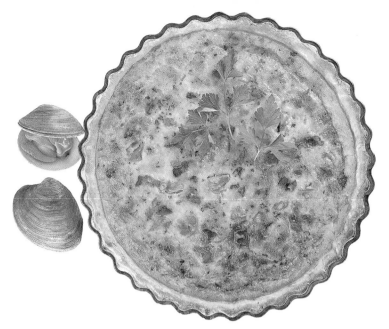

Clam Quiche with Bacon
(4 servings)

1	quiche shell	1
1 tbsp	butter	15 mL
1	onion, peeled and chopped	1
1½ cups	fresh clams, shucked, chopped and drained well	375 mL
6	slices crisp-cooked bacon, diced	6
¼ cup	grated Parmesan cheese	50 mL
1 cup	grated Gruyère cheese	250 mL
3	large eggs	3
1	large egg yolk	1
1 cup	heavy cream	250 mL
1 tbsp	chopped fresh parsley	15 mL
	egg wash	
	salt and freshly ground pepper	
	cayenne pepper to taste	

Preheat oven to 400°F (200°C).

1 Line dough with waxed or parchment paper. Fill with baking weights or dried beans. Precook 10 minutes in oven.

2 Remove paper and weights from dough. Prick bottom of dough with fork and brush with egg wash. Return to oven and cook 5 minutes. Remove and set mold aside.

3 Heat butter in frying pan over medium heat. Add onion and cook 3 minutes. Let cool, then transfer to precooked quiche shell.

4 Add chopped clams, bacon and both cheeses to quiche shell. Season well with pepper.

5 Mix all eggs and cream together; season well. Add parsley and cayenne pepper; mix again. Pour over cheese and bake quiche 25 to 30 minutes in oven.

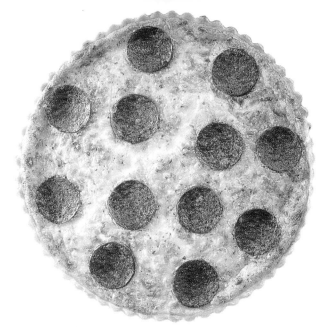

Ham and Pepperoni Quiche
(4 servings)

4	slices cooked ham, in julienne	4
12	slices pepperoni	12
1½ cups	grated mozzarella cheese	375 mL
1 tbsp	chopped fresh chervil	15 mL
3	large eggs	3
1	large egg yolk	1
1 cup	light cream	250 mL
	precooked quiche shell	
	salt and freshly ground pepper	

Preheat oven to 375°F (190°C).

1 Spread strips of ham and slices of pepperoni over bottom of quiche shell. Top with cheese and chervil.

2 Mix all eggs and cream together; season well. Pour over cheese and bake quiche 25 to 30 minutes in oven. Serve garnished with additional pepperoni slices, if desired.

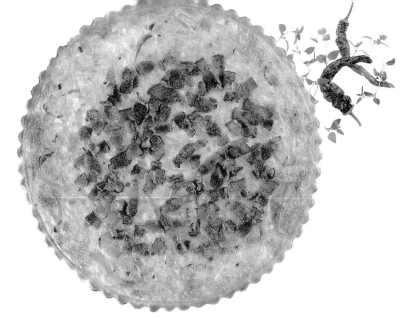

Leek and Bacon Quiche
(4 servings)

4	leeks, white part only	4
2 tbsp	butter	30 mL
6	slices crisp-cooked bacon, chopped	6
4	large eggs	4
1 cup	heavy cream	250 mL
1 cup	grated Emmenthal cheese	250 mL
	precooked quiche shell	
	salt and freshly ground pepper	
	pinch of nutmeg	

Preheat oven to 375°F (190°C).

1 Slit leeks from top to bottom twice, leaving 1 in (2.5 cm) intact at base. Wash leeks under cold, running water to remove grit and sand. Drain and slice thinly.

2 Heat butter in frying pan over medium heat. Add leeks, season and cook 12 minutes or until soft. Remove leeks from pan, drain well and set aside to cool slightly.

3 Spread leeks over bottom of quiche shell. Add bacon and season well.

4 Mix all eggs and cream together; season well. Pour over leeks and top with cheese. Sprinkle with nutmeg and bake quiche 25 to 30 minutes in oven. Serve garnished with crumbled bacon, if desired.

Roasted Bell Pepper Quiche
(4 servings)

3	large red bell peppers	3
½	jalapeño pepper, seeded and chopped	½
½ cup	grated Emmenthal cheese	125 mL
½ cup	grated Gruyère cheese	125 mL
3	large eggs	3
1	large egg yolk	1
1 cup	heavy cream	250 mL
	precooked quiche shell	
	salt and pepper	

1 Cut bell peppers in half and remove seeds. Oil skin and place cut-side-down on cookie sheet; broil 15 to 20 minutes in oven. Remove from oven and let cool. Peel off skin and place in food processor with jalapeño pepper. Blend to purée. Season mixture well.

2 Preheat oven to 375°F (190°C).

3 Spread puréed pepper mixture over bottom of quiche shell. Top with both cheeses.

4 Mix all eggs and cream together; season well. Pour over cheese and bake quiche 25 to 30 minutes in oven.

Bacon Quiche with Sharp Cheddar
(4 servings)

2 tbsp	butter	30 mL
4	onions, peeled and thinly sliced	4
6	slices crisp-cooked bacon, chopped	6
1 tbsp	chopped fresh parsley	15 mL
⅓ cup	grated Gruyère cheese	75 mL
¼ cup	grated sharp cheddar cheese	50 mL
3	large eggs	3
1	large egg yolk	1
1 cup	light cream	250 mL
	salt and freshly ground pepper	
	precooked quiche shell	

Preheat oven to 375°F (190°C).

1 Heat butter in frying pan over medium heat. Add onions and season well; cook 16 minutes over low heat. Be careful not to burn onions.

2 Spread onions over bottom of quiche shell. Add bacon, parsley and both cheeses.

3 Mix all eggs and cream together; season well. Pour over cheese and bake quiche 25 to 30 minutes in oven.

Eggplant Quiche
(4 servings)

I	large eggplant	I
2 tbsp	olive oil	30 mL
I	onion, peeled and chopped	I
I tbsp	chopped fresh basil	15 mL
I tbsp	chopped fresh parsley	15 mL
½	jalapeño pepper, seeded and chopped	½
⅓ cup	grated Parmesan cheese	75 mL
½ cup	grated Swiss cheese	125 mL
3	large eggs	3
¾ cup	light cream	175 mL
	salt and freshly ground pepper	
	precooked quiche shell	

Preheat oven to 400°F (200°C).

1 Slice eggplant in half lengthwise. Score flesh with knife in criss-cross pattern and brush with olive oil. Place, cut-side-down, on cookie sheet. Cook 40 minutes in oven. Scoop out flesh from shells, chop and set aside.

2 Heat remaining oil in frying pan over medium heat. Add onion and cook 4 minutes. Stir in eggplant, herbs and jalapeño pepper. Season well and cook 16 minutes over high heat to evaporate cooking liquid.

3 Transfer eggplant mixture to quiche shell and top with both cheeses.

4 Mix eggs and cream together; season well. Pour over cheese and bake quiche 25 to 30 minutes in oven.

Slice eggplant in half lengthwise. Score flesh with knife in criss-cross pattern and brush with olive oil.

Scoop out flesh from shells, chop and set aside.

Heat oil in frying pan over medium heat. Add onion and cook 4 minutes. Stir in eggplant, herbs and jalapeño pepper.

Transfer eggplant mixture to quiche shell and top with both cheeses.

Mix eggs and cream together; season well and pour over cheese.

Quiche Florentine
(4 servings)

2	bunches fresh spinach	2
2 tbsp	butter	30 mL
2	dry shallots, peeled and chopped	2
1 cup	grated Gruyère cheese	250 mL
2	large eggs	2
1	large egg yolk	1
1 cup	light cream	250 mL
	salt and pepper	
	precooked quiche shell	

Preheat oven to 375°F (190°C).

1 Remove thick stems from spinach. Wash leaves in plenty of cold water and cook, covered, in small amount of boiling water for 3 minutes. Transfer spinach to sieve and squeeze out excess water by pressing with back of spoon. Chop and set aside.

2 Heat butter in frying pan over medium heat. Add shallots and chopped spinach. Season well and cook 4 minutes.

3 Fill quiche shell with spinach and top with cheese.

4 Mix all eggs with cream and pour over cheese. Season well with pepper. Bake 25 to 30 minutes.

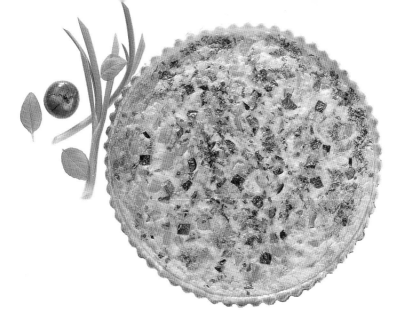

Zucchini Quiche with Lemon Zest
(4 servings)

2 tbsp	butter	30 mL
2	medium zucchini, diced	2
1 tbsp	chopped fresh basil	15 mL
1 tsp	grated lemon zest	5 mL
1	yellow bell pepper, finely diced	1
1¼ cups	grated Gruyère cheese	300 mL
3	large eggs	3
1	large egg yolk	1
1 cup	heavy cream	250 mL
	salt and pepper	
	precooked quiche shell	

Preheat oven to 375°F (190°C).

1 Heat butter in frying pan over medium heat. Add zucchini, basil, lemon zest and bell pepper. Season well and cook 6 minutes.

2 Remove pan from heat and let mixture cool. Fill quiche shell with vegetables and top with cheese.

3 Mix all eggs and cream together; season well. Pour over cheese and bake quiche 25 to 30 minutes in oven.

Basic Crêpe Batter

(yield: 14 to 16 crêpes)

1 cup	sifted all-purpose flour	250 mL
¼ tsp	salt	1 mL
1 tsp	vanilla	5 mL
3	large eggs, lightly beaten	3
2 cups	milk	500 mL
3 tbsp	melted butter	45 mL

1 Sift flour and salt into bowl.

2 Add vanilla to beaten eggs and whisk to incorporate. Pour over flour and mix well with wooden spoon.

3 Add milk and incorporate using whisk. Mix in butter.

4 Pass batter through sieve into clean bowl. Cover with sheet of plastic wrap touching surface and refrigerate 2 hours.

5 Bring to room temperature before using.

How to Make Crêpes

•

Crêpes are easier to make if you use a proper crêpe pan. If necessary substitute with a low-sided small frying pan.

•

Always bring the crêpe batter to room temperature before using.

•

Practice makes perfect. A properly made crêpe should be thin with an even consistency.

•

The temperature of the crêpe pan is crucial. You will need to adjust the heat as you go along. The pan should not be so hot that the butter burns.

•

Have a bowl of softened butter handy and use a piece of paper towel to quickly wipe butter onto the pan. How much butter you add and how often, will vary during the cooking process.

•

If you plan to refrigerate crêpes for later use, stack them with pieces of waxed paper between each.

•

Crêpes will keep for several days in the refrigerator.

Crêpe-Making Tips

Place crêpe pan over medium heat. When hot, use piece of paper towel to wipe pan with unsalted butter. Pour out any excess.

Return pan over medium heat. Add ladle of crêpe batter and holding pan above stove, rotate smoothly to spread batter evenly. Turn pan on a 90° angle and let excess batter drip back into bowl.

Return pan to stove and cook crêpe over medium-high heat until underside is golden brown. Using long metal spatula, turn crêpe over carefully and cook other side.

Remove pan from heat and let crêpe slide out onto large dinner plate. Stack crêpes on this plate as they are cooked.

Add more butter to pan, heat and repeat process.

Thin Crêpe Batter
(yield: 16 to 18 crêpes)

3 cups	milk	750 mL
2 cups	sifted all-purpose flour	500 mL
1¼ tsp	salt	6 mL
4	large eggs	4
3 tbsp	melted butter	45 mL

1 Pour milk into saucepan and boil 3 minutes. Pour milk through sieve into measuring cup.

2 Sift flour and salt into bowl. Add eggs and mix well with wooden spoon.

3 Pour in hot milk and whisk vigorously. Mix in butter.

4 Pass batter through clean sieve into clean bowl. Cover with sheet of plastic wrap touching surface. Refrigerate 2 hours.

5 Bring to room temperature before using.

Herb Crêpe Batter
(yield: 16 to 18 crêpes)

1 cup	all-purpose flour	250 mL
½ tsp	salt	2 mL
3	large eggs	3
1 cup	milk	250 mL
4 tbsp	melted butter	60 mL
2 tbsp	chopped fresh chives	30 mL
1 tbsp	chopped fresh parsley	15 mL
1 tbsp	chopped fresh tarragon	15 mL

1 Sift flour and salt into bowl.

2 Add eggs and mix with wooden spoon. Pour in milk; whisk to incorporate. Mix in butter.

3 Pass batter through sieve into clean bowl. Stir in herbs and cover with sheet of plastic wrap touching surface. Refrigerate 1 hour.

4 Bring to room temperature before using.

Buckwheat Crêpe Batter
(yield: 14 crêpes)

1½ cups	buckwheat flour	375 mL
½ tsp	salt	2 mL
¾ cup	cornmeal	175 mL
3	large eggs, beaten	3
2½ cups	milk	625 mL
3 tbsp	melted butter	45 mL

1 Sift flour, salt and cornmeal together into bowl.

2 Add beaten eggs and mix well with wooden spoon. Pour in milk and whisk to incorporate.

3 Stir in melted butter. Pass batter through sieve into clean bowl. Cover with sheet of plastic wrap touching surface and refrigerate 2 hours.

4 Bring to room temperature before using.

Dessert Crêpe Batter
(yield: 16 to 18 crêpes)

2 cups	sifted all-purpose flour	500 mL
½ cup	superfine sugar	125 mL
4	large eggs	4
1 tsp	vanilla	5 mL
2 cups	milk	500 mL
3 tbsp	brandy	45 mL
4 tbsp	melted butter	60 mL
	pinch of salt	

1 Sift flour and salt into bowl. Mix in sugar. Add eggs and mix well with wooden spoon.

2 Mix vanilla with milk; pour into bowl. Incorporate using whisk.

3 Add brandy and butter; mix well. Pass batter through sieve into clean bowl. Cover with sheet of plastic wrap touching surface and refrigerate 2 hours.

4 Bring to room temperature before using.

Blue Cheese-Filled Crêpes with Walnuts
(4 to 6 servings)

1 cup	blue cheese, crumbled	250 mL
3 tbsp	softened butter	45 mL
6	walnuts	6
	freshly ground pepper	
	cayenne pepper	
	few drops of Worcestershire sauce	
	crêpes	

1 Place cheese, butter, walnuts and all seasonings in food processor. Blend until smooth. Correct seasoning.

2 Spread thin layer of cheese filling over each crêpe. Roll up into tight cigar-like tube. Wrap in sheet of waxed paper and secure with string. Refrigerate 30 minutes.

3 Slice crêpes into ¾-in (2-cm) pieces. Arrange on platter and serve with drinks.

Prosciutto and Melon Crêpes
(4 to 6 servings)

4 tbsp	softened butter	60 mL
1 tsp	Dijon mustard	5 mL
12	crêpes	12
12	thin slices prosciutto	12
36	melon balls	36
	freshly ground pepper	

1 Mix butter with mustard. Spread over each crêpe and cover with prosciutto. Roll up into tight cigar-like tube. Wrap in sheet of waxed paper and secure with string. Refrigerate 30 minutes.

2 Slice crêpes into ¾-in (2-cm) pieces. Skewer melon balls and crêpe pieces with toothpicks. Arrange on platter and serve with drinks.

Fast Seafood Crêpes with Olives
(4 to 6 servings)

1 tbsp	olive oil	15 mL
3	green onions, chopped	3
2	garlic cloves, peeled, crushed and chopped	2
3	tomatoes, peeled, seeded and chopped	3
2 tbsp	chopped fresh basil	30 mL
24	marinated pitted black olives, chopped	24
7 oz	can tuna, drained and flaked	198 g
1 tbsp	chopped fresh parsley	15 mL
8	crêpes	8
⅓ cup	grated Parmesan cheese	75 mL
	salt and freshly ground pepper	

Preheat oven to 400°F (200°C).

1 Heat oil in frying pan over high heat. Add green onions and garlic; cook 2 minutes.

2 Add tomatoes and basil; season well. Cook 12 minutes over medium heat.

3 Mix in olives, tuna and parsley. Simmer 1 minute. Fill crêpes with mixture, roll and place in baking dish. Sprinkle with cheese and bake 8 minutes in oven.

Curried Shrimp Crêpes with Honey
(4 servings)

¼ cup	honey	50 mL
1 tbsp	curry powder	15 mL
1 tsp	Dijon mustard	5 mL
¾ lb	fresh shrimp, peeled, deveined and cut in three	350 g
1 tbsp	olive oil	15 mL
4	crêpes	4
1 cup	grated Gruyère cheese	250 mL
	salt and pepper	
	lemon juice	

Preheat oven to 400°F (200°C).

1 Mix honey, curry powder, mustard, salt, pepper and lemon juice together. Add shrimp to marinade and mix well.

2 Heat oil in frying pan over medium heat. Add shrimp and sauté 2 minutes over high heat.

3 Fill crêpes with mixture, roll and place in baking dish. Top with cheese and cook 4 minutes in oven. Serve.

Stuffed Shrimp and Mushroom Crêpes
(4 servings)

3 tbsp	butter	45 mL
½ lb	fresh shrimp, peeled and deveined	225 g
½ lb	fresh mushrooms, cleaned and halved	225 g
2	dry shallots, peeled and finely chopped	2
1 tbsp	chopped fresh tarragon	15 mL
2 tbsp	flour	30 mL
1 cup	milk, heated	250 mL
½ cup	grated Gruyère cheese	125 mL
8	crêpes	8
	salt and freshly ground pepper	
	Parmesan cheese (optional)	

1 Heat butter in sauté pan over medium heat. Add shrimp and sauté 2 to 3 minutes. Remove shrimp from pan and set aside.

2 Add mushrooms, shallots and tarragon. Season well and continue cooking 4 minutes.

3 Reduce heat to low. Sprinkle in flour and mix well. Cook 1 minute. Pour in milk and season well. Mix and cook 6 minutes over low heat.

4 Stir in shrimp and cheese. Divide mixture among crêpes, roll and place on ovenproof platter. Sprinkle with Parmesan cheese, if desired. Broil 2 minutes in oven and serve.

Hungarian Crêpes
(4 servings)

1 lb	fresh spinach	450 g
4 tbsp	butter	60 mL
1	large dry shallot, peeled and chopped	1
2	tomatoes, peeled, seeded and chopped	2
2	hard-boiled eggs, sliced	2
8	crêpes (buckwheat, optional)	8
½ cup	grated Parmesan cheese	125 mL
	salt and freshly ground pepper	

Preheat oven to 400°F (200°C).

1 Remove stems from spinach. Wash leaves well and cook in ½ cup (125 mL) of boiling water for 4 minutes. Transfer spinach to sieve and squeeze out excess water by pressing with back of spoon. Chop and set aside.

2 Heat half of butter in sauté pan over medium heat. Add shallot and cook 2 minutes. Add chopped spinach and season well. Cook 5 minutes over high heat.

3 Stir in tomatoes, season and continue cooking 8 minutes.

4 Incorporate sliced eggs and fill crêpes with mixture. Roll and place crêpes in baking dish. Melt remaining butter and drizzle over crêpes. Top with cheese and bake 5 minutes in oven.

Crêpes with Mussels in White Wine Sauce
(4 servings)

3 lb	fresh mussels, bearded and scrubbed	1.4 kg
½ cup	dry white wine	125 mL
1 tbsp	chopped fresh parsley	15 mL
3 tbsp	butter	45 mL
2	dry shallots, peeled and chopped	2
½ lb	fresh mushrooms, cleaned and diced	225 g
1½ cups	white sauce, heated (see page 90)	375 mL
8	crêpes	8
½ cup	grated Gruyère cheese	125 mL
	salt and freshly ground pepper	

Preheat oven to 400°F (200°C).

1 Place mussels in large pan. Add wine and parsley. Cover and bring to boil. Cook mussels over low heat until shells open, about 5 minutes. Stir once during cooking.

2 Remove mussels from pan, discarding any unopened shells. Detach mussels from shells and set aside. Pass cooking liquid through sieve lined with cheesecloth into small saucepan. Cook 4 minutes over medium heat. Set aside.

3 Heat butter in sauté pan over medium heat. Add shallots and mushrooms; season well. Cook 4 minutes.

4 Add mussels, white sauce and reserved cooking liquid. Mix well and simmer 2 minutes.

5 Fill crêpes with mixture. Fold in four and place crêpes in baking dish. Cover with remaining sauce and top with cheese. Cook 6 minutes in oven.

Seafood Crêpes
(4 servings)

3 tbsp	butter	45 mL
¾ lb	fresh scallops, cleaned	350 g
1	dry shallot, peeled and chopped	1
½ lb	fresh mushrooms, cleaned and diced	225 g
1 tbsp	chopped fresh parsley	15 mL
1 tsp	tarragon	5 mL
1 cup	clam juice	250 mL
2 tbsp	flour	30 mL
½ cup	grated mozzarella cheese	125 mL
8	crêpes	8
	salt and pepper	
	cayenne pepper to taste	

Preheat oven to 375°F (190°C).

1 Grease frying pan lightly with some of butter. Add scallops, shallot, mushrooms and all seasonings to pan. Pour in clam juice and cover with sheet of waxed paper.

2 Bring to boiling point over medium heat. Reduce heat to low and simmer 2 minutes. Remove pan from heat.

3 Using slotted spoon, transfer scallops and mushrooms to bowl. Return pan to stove and boil remaining liquid 4 minutes.

4 Heat remaining butter in saucepan over low heat. Sprinkle in flour and mix well. Cook 1 minute. Pour in reduced cooking liquid from scallops and whisk to incorporate. Season well and cook sauce 3 minutes over low heat.

5 Stir in cheese, scallops and mushrooms. Simmer 1 to 2 minutes.

6 Spoon most of seafood mixture on crêpes, roll and place in baking dish. Pour remaining sauce over crêpes and bake 4 minutes in oven.

Creamy Mushroom-Stuffed Crêpes
(4 servings)

2 tbsp	olive oil	30 mL
1 lb	fresh mushrooms, cleaned and sliced in three	450 g
3	green onions, chopped	3
1	garlic clove, peeled, crushed and chopped	1
1 tbsp	curry powder	15 mL
1½ cups	white sauce, heated (see page 90)	375 mL
1 tbsp	chopped fresh chives	15 mL
1 cup	grated Gruyère cheese	250 mL
8	crêpes	8
	salt and pepper	
	pinch of nutmeg	

1 Heat oil in frying pan over high heat. Add mushrooms, season and cook 3 minutes. Add onions and garlic; cook 1 minute.

2 Reduce heat to medium. Sprinkle in curry powder and mix well. Incorporate white sauce, chives, cheese and nutmeg. Correct seasoning. Cook 3 minutes.

3 Divide most of mixture between crêpes, roll and place in baking dish. Cover with remaining sauce. Broil 8 minutes in oven.

Breakfast Crêpes
(4 servings)

4	pork sausages	4
1 tbsp	butter	15 mL
4	eggs	4
4	crêpes	4
½ cup	grated Emmenthal cheese	125 mL
	salt and pepper	

1 Place sausages in boiling water and cook 2 minutes. Remove and drain well.

2 Heat butter in frying pan over medium heat. Add sausages and cook 5 minutes over low heat.

3 When sausages are cooked, remove from pan and set aside. Break eggs into hot frying pan, season and cook 3 to 4 minutes.

4 Fill each crêpe with fried egg and sausage. Fold in half and place on ovenproof platter. Top with grated cheese.

5 Broil 2 minutes in oven and serve with toast.

Lobster Crêpes with Tarragon White Wine Sauce
(4 servings)

3 tbsp	butter	45 mL
1 lb	fresh lobster meat, diced	450 g
2	dry shallots, peeled and chopped	2
¾ lb	fresh mushrooms, cleaned and diced	350 g
½ cup	dry white wine	125 mL
1 cup	clam juice	250 mL
1 tbsp	chopped fresh tarragon	15 mL
1 tbsp	cornstarch	15 mL
3 tbsp	cold water	45 mL
8	crêpes	8
¼ cup	grated Parmesan cheese	50 mL
	salt and pepper	

Preheat oven to 375°F (190°C).

1 Heat butter in frying pan over medium heat. Add lobster meat and shallots; season with pepper. Cook 2 minutes. Remove lobster meat from pan and set aside.

2 Add mushrooms to hot pan and season well. Cook 5 minutes over high heat. Pour in wine and continue cooking 2 minutes.

3 Stir in clam juice and tarragon. Cook 3 minutes over medium heat.

4 Reduce heat to low. Dilute cornstarch in cold water; stir into sauce. Add lobster meat and simmer 2 minutes.

5 Divide mixture between crêpes, roll and place in baking dish. Sprinkle with cheese and cook 8 minutes in oven.

Last Minute Cheese Crêpes
(4 servings)

8	crêpes	8
1½ cups	Egg Sauce, heated (see page 91)	375 mL
½ cup	grated Gruyère cheese	125 mL
½ cup	grated cheddar cheese	125 mL
¼ cup	grated Emmenthal cheese	50 mL
	freshly ground pepper	

Preheat oven to 400°F (200°C).

1 Lay crêpes flat on work surface. Spread 1 tbsp (15 mL) of egg sauce over each crêpe. Sprinkle with grated cheeses and season with pepper.

2 Roll crêpes and place in buttered baking dish. Cover with remaining egg sauce and top with remaining cheese. Bake 12 minutes.

Julienne-Stuffed Crêpes with White Sauce
(4 servings)

2 tbsp	butter	30 mL
2	onions, peeled and sliced	2
3	slices cooked ham, in julienne	3
2	slices Gruyère cheese, in julienne	2
½ cup	white sauce, heated (see page 90)	125 mL
4	crêpes	4
	freshly ground pepper	

1 Heat butter in frying pan over medium heat. Add onions and cook 12 minutes over low heat. Do not allow onions to burn.

2 Remove onions from pan and set aside.

3 Divide ham, cheese, cooked onions and white sauce between crêpes. Season with freshly ground pepper. Fold crêpes in four and place on ovenproof platter.

4 Broil 2 to 3 minutes in oven or until hot. Serve.

Crêpes Stuffed with Fillet of Sole
(4 servings)

2 tbsp	butter	30 mL
1	onion, peeled and sliced	1
½ lb	fresh mushrooms, cleaned and sliced	225 g
2	sole fillets	2
½ cup	dry white wine	125 mL
½ cup	water	125 mL
8	crêpes	8
½ cup	thick white sauce, heated (see page 90)	125 mL
1 tbsp	chopped fresh parsley	15 mL
	salt and freshly ground pepper	
	pinch of paprika	

1 Heat butter in frying pan over medium heat. Add onion and cook 2 minutes. Increase heat to high and add mushrooms. Season well and cook 2 minutes.

2 Place sole in pan. Pour in wine and water. Season well and cover with sheet of waxed paper touching surface. Bring to boil.

3 As soon as liquid starts to boil, remove pan from stove. Let fish stand 2 minutes in hot liquid.

4 Remove fish and mushrooms from pan using slotted spoon. Divide between crêpes; set aside.

5 Return pan to stove and cook liquid over high heat until reduced by ⅓. Mix in white sauce and paprika. Add about 3 tbsp (45 mL) of sauce to each crêpe.

6 Fold crêpes in four and place in baking dish. Top with remaining sauce and broil 2 minutes in oven. Sprinkle with parsley and serve.

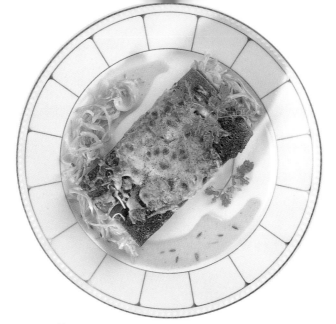

Cabbage and Onion Baked Crêpes
(4 servings)

1 tbsp	olive oil	15 mL
1	onion, peeled and thinly sliced	1
2 cups	shredded cabbage	500 mL
2 tbsp	white wine	30 mL
¼ tsp	sugar	1 mL
1	recipe Egg Sauce, heated (see page 91)	1
8	crêpes (buckwheat, optional)	8
½ cup	grated Swiss cheese	125 mL
	salt and freshly ground pepper	
	pinch of caraway seeds	
	pinch of paprika	

Preheat oven to 400°F (200°C).

1 Heat oil in frying pan over medium heat. Add onion and cook 4 minutes. Stir in cabbage and season well. Cover and cook 6 minutes.

2 Add wine, sugar, caraway seeds, salt, pepper and paprika. Mix well, cover and cook 15 minutes over low heat. Stir occasionally.

3 Incorporate 1 cup (250 mL) of egg sauce to cabbage mixture. Fill crêpes, roll and place in baking dish. Cover with remaining egg sauce.

4 Top with cheese and bake 12 minutes in oven.

Crêpes with Ground Veal and Mornay Sauce
(4 servings)

2 tbsp	butter	30 mL
1	onion, peeled and chopped	1
½	celery rib, chopped	½
½ lb	fresh mushrooms, cleaned and diced	225 g
1 tbsp	chopped fresh basil	15 mL
1 tbsp	chopped fresh parsley	15 mL
¾ lb	ground veal	350 g
2 cups	Mornay Sauce, warm (see page 90)	500 mL
8	crêpes	8
¾ cup	grated Emmenthal cheese	175 mL
	salt and pepper	

Preheat oven to 400°F (200°C).

1 Heat butter in frying pan over medium heat. Add onion and celery; cook 3 to 4 minutes. Add mushrooms and seasonings; mix well. Continue cooking 4 minutes.

2 Add ground veal and season generously. Brown 3 minutes over medium-high heat.

3 When meat is cooked, stir in Mornay Sauce. Simmer 1 minute, then remove pan from heat. Fill crêpes with most of mixture, roll and place in baking dish.

4 Cover with remaining veal sauce and top with cheese. Cook 5 to 6 minutes in oven.

Crêpes Tropicana
(4 servings)

1	whole boneless chicken breast	1
2 cups	light chicken stock, heated	500 mL
3 tbsp	butter	45 mL
1	onion, peeled and finely diced	1
1 tbsp	curry powder	15 mL
3 tbsp	flour	45 mL
2	pineapple rings, diced	2
½	banana, sliced on the bias	½
8	crêpes	8
2 tbsp	grated Parmesan cheese	30 mL
	salt and pepper	

Preheat oven to 375°F (190°C).

1 Skin chicken breast and split into two. Place in sauté pan with chicken stock. Bring to boil. Reduce heat to low and cook 12 to 15 minutes or adjust time according to size.

2 When cooked, remove chicken from liquid and let cool 2 minutes. Dice meat and set aside. Reserve chicken stock separately.

3 Heat butter in saucepan over medium heat. Add onion and cook 2 minutes. Sprinkle in curry powder, mix well and cook 2 minutes over low heat.

4 Mix in flour, then pour in reserved chicken stock. Season well and whisk to incorporate. Cook sauce 8 minutes over low heat.

5 Add diced chicken, pineapple and banana to sauce. Mix well and simmer 2 minutes.

6 Place about 3 tbsp (45 mL) of chicken mixture on each crêpe. Fold in four and place crêpes in baking dish. Cover with remaining sauce. Sprinkle with cheese and bake 6 minutes in oven.

Crêpes Stuffed with Ham and Cheese
(2 servings)

4	crêpes	4
4	thick slices Black Forest ham	4
1 cup	grated Gruyère cheese	250 mL
	freshly ground pepper	

1 Lay crêpes flat on work surface. Cover with ham and top with grated cheese. Season generously with pepper.

2 Fold crêpes in four and place on ovenproof platter.

3 Broil 2 minutes in oven or until hot. Serve.

Crêpes with Spinach and Mornay Sauce
(4 servings)

1½ lb	fresh spinach	675 g
2 tbsp	butter	30 mL
4	slices prosciutto ham, in julienne	4
2 cups	Mornay Sauce, warm (see page 90)	500 mL
8	crêpes	8
½ cup	grated Gruyère cheese	125 mL
	salt and freshly ground pepper	
	pinch of nutmeg	

Preheat oven to 375°F (190°C).

1 Remove stems from spinach. Wash leaves and cook in small amount of boiling water for 3 minutes or until wilted. Transfer spinach to sieve and squeeze out excess water by pressing with back of spoon. Chop spinach.

2 Heat butter in sauté pan over medium heat. Add chopped spinach and prosciutto; season and add nutmeg. Cook 3 minutes.

3 Add Mornay Sauce and mix well. Divide most of mixture between crêpes, roll and place in baking dish. Cover with remaining Mornay mixture. Top with cheese and bake 8 minutes in oven.

Braised Endive Crêpe Entrée
(4 servings)

2 tbsp	butter	30 mL
4	large endives, cored	4
½ cup	chicken stock, heated	125 mL
1 cup	white sauce, heated (see page 90)	250 mL
4	crêpes	4
½ cup	grated Emmenthal cheese	125 mL
	juice of ½ lemon	
	salt and freshly ground pepper	

Preheat oven to 375°F (190°C).

1 Grease baking dish with butter. Place endives in dish and sprinkle with lemon juice. Season well and pour in chicken stock. Cook 35 minutes in oven or until tender.

2 Remove endives from baking dish and drain well on paper towel; set aside. Pour cooking liquid into small saucepan and cook 3 minutes over high heat. Stir in white sauce and season well. Simmer 1 minute over low heat.

3 Place one endive on each crêpe. Roll and place in baking dish. Cover with sauce and top with cheese. Broil 6 minutes in oven.

Hearty Italian Crêpe Casserole
(4 to 6 servings)

2	small eggplants	2
3 tbsp	olive oil	45 mL
1	onion, peeled and chopped	1
2	garlic cloves, peeled, crushed and chopped	2
3	tomatoes, peeled, seeded and chopped	3
12	crêpes	12
8	slices mozzarella cheese	8
4	slices prosciutto, in julienne	4
¼ cup	grated Parmesan cheese	50 mL
	salt and freshly ground pepper	
	melted butter	

1 Slice eggplants ¼ in (5 mm) thick and arrange in single layer on large tray. Sprinkle with salt and let stand 2 hours at room temperature. Drain off juices, rinse away salt and pat dry with paper towels.

2 Preheat oven to 375°F (190°C).

3 Place eggplant slices on oven-proof tray and brush lightly with olive oil. Cook 16 minutes in oven.

4 Meanwhile, heat remaining oil in frying pan over medium heat. Add onion and garlic; cook 5 minutes. Stir in tomatoes, season and cook 12 minutes.

5 Reduce oven temperature to 350°F (180°C).

6 Line sides and bottom of buttered baking dish with half of crêpes. Add layers of eggplant, mozzarella cheese, prosciutto and tomatoes. Season well and repeat each layer once.

7 Sprinkle with Parmesan cheese and cover with remaining crêpes. Drizzle with melted butter. Bake 20 minutes in oven. If crêpes brown too quickly, cover loosely with foil. Let stand several minutes before serving.

Place eggplant slices on ovenproof tray and brush lightly with olive oil. Cook 16 minutes in oven.

Heat oil in frying pan over medium heat. Add onion and garlic; cook 5 minutes. Stir in tomatoes, season and cook 12 minutes.

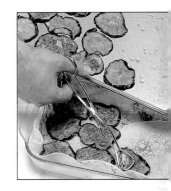

Line sides and bottom of buttered baking dish with half of crêpes. Add layer of eggplant.

Add layers of mozzarella cheese, prosciutto and tomatoes. Season well and repeat each layer once.

Sprinkle with Parmesan cheese and cover with remaining crêpes.

Crêpes Stuffed with Roquefort Cheese
(4 servings)

½ cup	white sauce, heated (see page 90)	125 mL
3 tbsp	Roquefort cheese, crumbled	45 mL
8	crêpes	8
2 tbsp	grated Parmesan cheese	30 mL
	pinch of nutmeg	
	freshly ground pepper	

Preheat oven to 400°F (200°C).

1 Mix white sauce with Roquefort cheese. Add nutmeg and blend until smooth.

2 Spread cheese mixture over crêpes and season with pepper. Roll and place in baking dish.

3 Top with Parmesan cheese and cook 6 minutes in oven.

Sauté of Summer Vegetables in Crêpes
(4 servings)

2 tbsp	olive oil	30 mL
1	onion, peeled and sliced	1
2	dry shallots, peeled and sliced	2
1	garlic clove, peeled, crushed and chopped	1
1	red bell pepper, sliced	1
2	tomatoes, peeled, seeded and chopped	2
1 tbsp	chopped fresh basil	15 mL
1 cup	grated Emmenthal cheese	250 mL
8	crêpes	8
	salt and freshly ground pepper	

1 Heat oil in frying pan over medium heat. Add onion and shallots; season and cook 8 minutes over low heat.

2 Stir in garlic, bell pepper and tomatoes. Season well and increase heat to medium. Cook 8 minutes.

3 Add basil and cheese. Cook 1 minute, then remove pan from heat and let cool 1 minute.

4 Spread mixture over crêpes, roll and place in baking dish. Broil 3 minutes in oven and serve.

Crêpes with Salmon in White Sauce
(4 to 6 servings)

3 tbsp	butter	45 mL
2	dry shallots, peeled and chopped	2
½ lb	fresh mushrooms, cleaned and sliced	225 g
½ cup	dry white wine	125 mL
2	fresh salmon steaks, cooked, boned and flaked	2
2 cups	white sauce, heated (see page 90)	500 mL
8 – 12	crêpes	8 – 12
½ cup	grated Gruyère cheese	125 mL
	salt and freshly ground pepper	
	paprika to taste	

Preheat oven to 400°F (200°C).

1 Heat butter in sauté pan over medium heat. Add shallots and mushrooms; season well. Cook 6 minutes over high heat. Pour in wine and continue cooking 2 minutes.

2 Stir in salmon and white sauce. Season generously with salt, pepper and paprika. Reduce heat to low and simmer 2 minutes.

3 Spoon about 3 tbsp (45 mL) of mixture on each crêpe. Roll and place crêpes in baking dish. Cover with remaining salmon mixture and top with cheese. Bake 8 minutes in oven.

Chicken and Avocado Crêpes
(4 servings)

1	avocado	1
3 tbsp	butter	45 mL
1	onion, peeled and finely chopped	1
1 tbsp	chopped fresh chives	15 mL
3 tbsp	flour	45 mL
2 cups	milk, heated	500 mL
2 cups	diced cooked chicken	500 mL
4 tbsp	grated Parmesan cheese	60 mL
8	crêpes	8
	lemon juice	
	salt and freshly ground pepper	

Preheat oven to 375°F (190°C).

1 Cut avocado in half lengthwise. Twist halves apart and remove pit. Peel and dice flesh. Toss with lemon juice and set aside.

2 Heat butter in saucepan over medium heat. Add onion and chives; cook 2 minutes over low heat.

3 Sprinkle in flour and mix well. Cook 1 minute. Pour in milk and whisk to incorporate. Season well and cook sauce 8 minutes over low heat. Stir in chicken, cheese and avocado. Simmer 2 minutes.

4 Spoon about 4 tbsp (60 mL) of chicken mixture on each crêpe. Roll and place in baking dish. Pour remaining chicken mixture over crêpes and cook 5 minutes in oven. Serve.

Seafood Crêpes with Emmenthal Cheese
(4 servings)

1 tbsp	olive oil	15 mL
12	shrimp, peeled and deveined	12
12	scallops, cleaned	12
12	mussels, cooked and shelled	12
2	dry shallots, peeled and chopped	2
1 tbsp	chopped fresh tarragon	15 mL
½ cup	dry white wine	125 mL
1½ cups	white sauce, heated (see page 90)	375 mL
½ cup	grated Emmenthal cheese	125 mL
8	crêpes	8
	salt and freshly ground pepper	
	paprika to taste	

Preheat oven to 425°F (220°C).

1 Heat oil in frying pan over high heat. Add shrimp and season with pepper. Cook 2 minutes.

2 Add scallops and continue cooking 2 minutes. Add mussels, mix well, and simmer 1 minute over low heat. Remove seafood from pan and set aside.

3 Add shallots and tarragon to hot pan; cook 2 minutes. Increase heat to high and pour in wine. Cook 2 minutes.

4 Stir in white sauce, paprika and half of cheese. Return seafood to pan, mix well and simmer 1 minute over low heat.

5 Fill crêpes with seafood mixture. Fold in four and place crêpes in baking dish. Top with remaining cheese and cook 4 minutes in oven. Serve.

Crêpes Stuffed with Steak and Mushrooms
(4 servings)

2 tbsp	olive oil	30 mL
2	8 oz (225 g) strip loin steaks, thinly sliced	2
½ lb	fresh mushrooms, cleaned and sliced	225 g
1	dry shallot, peeled and chopped	1
½ cup	dry red wine	125 mL
1 cup	beef stock, heated	250 mL
1 tbsp	cornstarch	15 mL
3 tbsp	cold water	45 mL
1 tbsp	chopped fresh parsley	15 mL
8	crêpes	8
	salt and pepper	

1 Heat half of oil in frying pan over medium heat. Season meat well with pepper and add to pan. Cook 1 minute over high heat. Remove meat from pan and set aside.

2 Add remaining oil to hot pan. Add mushrooms and shallot; season well. Cook 4 minutes over medium heat. Pour in wine and cook 2 minutes over high heat.

3 Stir in beef stock and continue cooking 2 minutes. Reduce heat to low. Dilute cornstarch in cold water; stir into sauce. Cook 1 minute, then add parsley.

4 Place meat in sauce and simmer 2 minutes. Stuff crêpes with mixture, fold in four and place in baking dish. Broil 2 minutes in oven and serve.

Tomato and Zucchini Crêpes
(4 servings)

1 tbsp	olive oil	15 mL
2	dry shallots, peeled and chopped	2
2	garlic cloves, peeled, crushed and chopped	2
1	small zucchini, finely diced	1
½ cup	dry white wine	125 mL
3	tomatoes, peeled, seeded and diced	3
2 tbsp	chopped fresh basil	30 mL
½ cup	grated Parmesan cheese	125 mL
8	crêpes	8
	salt and freshly ground pepper	

1 Heat oil in frying pan over medium heat. Add shallots, garlic and zucchini. Season well and cook 3 minutes over low heat.

2 Increase heat to high. Pour in wine and cook 2 minutes. Stir in tomatoes and basil; season well. Cook 6 minutes.

3 Reduce heat to medium and stir in cheese. Cook 3 minutes, then remove pan from heat. Let stuffing cool slightly.

4 Spread mixture over crêpes, roll and place on ovenproof platter. Broil 3 minutes in oven and serve.

Vegetable-Stuffed Crêpes with Egg Sauce
(4 servings)

1 tbsp	olive oil	15 mL
3	green onions, chopped	3
1	carrot, pared and finely diced	1
1	zucchini, finely diced	1
1	yellow bell pepper, finely diced	1
1	garlic clove, peeled, crushed and chopped	1
1 tbsp	chopped fresh basil	15 mL
2	large tomatoes, peeled, seeded and chopped	2
½ cup	grated Emmenthal cheese	125 mL
8	crêpes	8
½	recipe Egg Sauce, heated (see page 91)	½
¾ cup	grated Gruyère cheese	175 mL
	salt and pepper	
	pinch of paprika	

Preheat oven to 425°F (220°C).

1 Heat oil in frying pan over high heat. Add vegetables, season and cook 6 minutes over medium heat. Add garlic and basil; continue cooking 2 minutes.

2 Stir in tomatoes and season well. Cook 6 minutes over high heat. Mix in Emmenthal cheese.

3 Fill crêpes with mixture and roll. Place in baking dish and cover with egg sauce. Top with grated Gruyère cheese and pinch of paprika. Cook 8 minutes in oven.

Soufflé Crêpes with Rum Cream
(4 to 6 servings)

SOUFFLÉ:

6	egg whites	6
½ lb	confectioners' sugar	225 g
8	crêpes	8
	grated zest of 1 orange	
	grated zest of ½ lemon	

Preheat oven to 475°F (240°C).

1 Beat egg whites until stiff. Add sugar and continue beating until very stiff. Gently fold in fruit zest.

2 Divide soufflé mixture among crêpes, fold in four and place on ovenproof platter. Bake 6 minutes and serve with Rum Cream Sauce.

RUM CREAM SAUCE:

6	egg yolks	6
⅓ cup	granulated sugar	75 mL
1 cup	light cream	250 mL
3 tbsp	rum	45 mL

1 Place egg yolks and sugar in stainless steel bowl. Beat 1 minute with electric hand mixer.

2 Place bowl over saucepan containing boiling water. Add cream and cook, stirring constantly, until thickened.

3 Stir in rum and serve warm over soufflé crêpes.

Fresh Peach Crêpe Cake
(6 to 8 servings)

1 lb	fresh peaches, pitted and peeled	450 g
1 cup	water	250 mL
4 tbsp	granulated sugar	60 mL
14	crêpes	14
2 tbsp	apricot jam	30 mL
2 tbsp	toasted sliced almonds	30 mL
	juice of ¼ lemon	
	grated zest of ½ lemon	

Preheat oven to 400°F (200°C).

1 Slice peaches and toss with lemon juice; set aside.

2 Place water, sugar and lemon zest in saucepan over medium heat. Cook 8 minutes. Add sliced peaches and continue cooking 7 minutes.

3 Remove pan from heat, mix well and let cool.

4 To make cake, place first crêpe flat on ovenproof platter. Add layer of peaches and position next crêpe. Repeat until all ingredients are used, ending with crêpe.

5 Spread jam over top crêpe and sprinkle with almonds. Bake 8 minutes in oven. Let cool slightly, slice in wedges and serve.

Crêpes aux Poires
(4 servings)

2	pears, cored, peeled and sliced	2
2	bananas, peeled and sliced	2
4 tbsp	superfine sugar	60 mL
1 cup	fresh raspberries	250 mL
8	crêpes	8
	grated zest of ¼ lemon	

1 Place pears, bananas and lemon zest in small saucepan. Add half of sugar and cook 8 minutes over medium heat.

2 Remove pan from heat and set aside to cool.

3 Place raspberries in food processor. Blend to purée. Add 1 tbsp (15 mL) sugar and mix well. Divide sauce among 4 dessert plates and set aside.

4 Fill crêpes with pear mixture and fold in four. Place on ovenproof platter and sprinkle with remaining sugar. Broil 3 minutes in oven.

5 Place each stuffed crêpe on pool of raspberry sauce. Serve at once.

Grand Marnier Crêpes with Raspberries
(4 to 6 servings)

5 tbsp	Grand Marnier (orange liqueur)	75 mL
¼ lb	soft cream cheese	125 g
12 – 18	crêpes	12 – 18
2 cups	fresh raspberries	500 mL
4 tbsp	superfine sugar	60 mL

1 Mix 1 tbsp (15 mL) liqueur with cream cheese. Spread small amount of cheese on each crêpe and fold in four. Place on ovenproof platter and broil 1 to 2 minutes or until lightly browned.

2 Meanwhile, place raspberries, sugar and remaining liqueur in saucepan. Cook 1 minute over medium heat.

3 Pour raspberries over crêpes and flambé. Serve.

Chestnut Cream Crêpes
(4 servings)

8 oz	canned sweetened chestnut purée	225 g
3 tbsp	rum	45 mL
1 ½ cups	whipped cream	375 mL
8	crêpes	8
	superfine sugar	

Preheat oven to 400°F (200°C).

1 Place chestnut purée in food processor; blend 1 minute. Pour in rum and blend briefly. Transfer mixture to bowl.

2 Fold in whipped cream and spread filling over crêpes. Roll and place crêpes on ovenproof platter. Sprinkle with sugar and cook 4 minutes in oven. Serve.

Berry Crêpes
(6 to 8 servings)

1 lb	fresh strawberries, washed and hulled	450 g
3 tbsp	superfine sugar	45 mL
½	recipe Dessert Cream Filling (see page 94)	½
12	crêpes	12

1 Place strawberries in food processor. Add 2 tbsp (30 mL) sugar and blend to purée. Divide ¾ of berry sauce among 6 dessert plates and set aside.

2 Place 2 tbsp (30 mL) of dessert cream filling on each crêpe. Add a small amount of strawberry purée to each crêpe. Roll and place on ovenproof platter. Sprinkle with remaining sugar and broil 3 minutes in oven.

3 Place each stuffed crêpe on pool of berry sauce. Serve at once.

Apple Brandy Crêpes with Apricot Jam
(4 to 6 servings)

APPLES:

3 tbsp	butter	45 mL
5	apples, cored, peeled and sliced	5
1 tsp	cinnamon	5 mL
⅓ cup	brown sugar	75 mL
1 tbsp	brandy	15 mL

1 Heat butter in frying pan over medium heat. Add apples, cinnamon and brown sugar. Cook 5 minutes.

2 Mix well and cover pan. Continue cooking 7 minutes.

3 Remove cover and pour in brandy. Increase heat to high and cook 3 minutes. Remove from heat and set aside.

APRICOT JAM:

1 cup	apricot jam	250 mL
1 cup	water	250 mL
1 tsp	cornstarch	5 mL
12	crêpes	12
	grated zest of 1 orange	

Preheat oven to 375°F (190°C).

1 Place jam in saucepan and pour in ¾ cup (175 mL) water. Add orange zest and bring to boil. Cook 2 minutes.

2 Dilute cornstarch in remaining water. Add to saucepan and mix well. Reduce heat to low and cook 1 minute.

3 Spread jam mixture and brandy apples between crêpes and stack on ovenproof platter. Bake 8 to 10 minutes. Slice and serve.

Heat butter in frying pan over medium heat. Add apples, brown sugar and cinnamon. Cook 5 minutes.

Pour in brandy. Increase heat to high and cook 3 minutes.

Place jam in saucepan and pour in ¾ cup (175 mL) water.

Spread jam mixture and brandy apples between crêpes.

Stack on ovenproof platter.

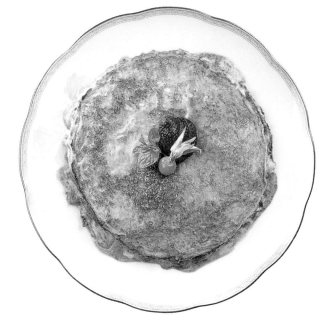

Tea Time Crêpes
(4 servings)

16	thin dessert crêpes	16
1½ cups	whipped cream	375 mL
½ cup	cherry jam	125 mL
3 tbsp	superfine sugar	45 mL
¼ cup	Cointreau (orange liqueur), heated	50 mL

1 Each serving requires a stack of 4 crêpes. Between each crêpe, alternate layers of whipped cream and cherry jam. Sprinkle top crêpe with sugar only.

2 Place stacks of crêpes flat on large ovenproof platter and broil 3 minutes in oven.

3 Serve with warm liqueur.

Apple Crêpe Galettes
(4 servings)

8	crêpes	8
2 tbsp	melted butter	30 mL
3	apples, cored, peeled and thinly sliced	3
½ cup	heavy cream	125 mL
½ cup	superfine sugar	125 mL

1 Arrange 4 crêpes flat on oven-proof platter. Brush with melted butter. Position remaining crêpes on top and brush with rest of butter.

2 Cover crêpes with apple slices, placed in fan-like shape. Drizzle cream over apples and sprinkle with sugar.

3 Broil 5 to 6 minutes in oven and serve.

Crêpes with Pastry Cream and Raspberries
(6 to 8 servings)

½ lb	fresh raspberries, cleaned	225 g
3 tbsp	granulated sugar	45 mL
12 – 16	crêpes	12 – 16
1	recipe Pastry Cream (see page 92)	1
	extra granulated sugar	

Preheat oven to 400°F (200°C).

1 Place raspberries and sugar in food processor. Blend for 20 seconds to purée.

2 Spread raspberries over crêpes and top with several spoonfuls of pastry cream.

3 Roll crêpes and place on oven-proof platter. Sprinkle with sugar and cook 6 minutes in oven.

Last Minute Maple Crêpes
(4 to 6 servings)

8	crêpes	8
2 tbsp	superfine sugar	30 mL
	pure maple syrup	

1 Sprinkle each crêpe with sugar.

2 Roll up into tight cigar-like tubes. Place on ovenproof platter.

3 Drizzle maple syrup over crêpes and dust with more sugar.

4 Broil in oven until edges turn brown. Serve with ice cream.

Crêpes Sultanes
(4 servings)

⅓ cup	apricot jam	75 mL
8	crêpes	8
2	bananas, sliced	2
4	pineapple rings, diced	4
2 tbsp	superfine sugar	30 mL
3 tbsp	rum	45 mL

Preheat oven to 450°F (230°C).

1 Spread thin layer of jam over each crêpe. Divide bananas and pineapple among crêpes. Fold in four and place on ovenproof platter.

2 Sprinkle with sugar and cook 6 minutes in oven.

3 Remove from oven and pour rum over crêpes, flambé and serve. Accompany with an apricot coulis, if desired.

Crêpes Filled with Hazelnut Butter
(4 servings)

1 cup	shelled hazelnuts	250 mL
¾ cup	unsalted butter	175 mL
¾ cup	confectioners' sugar	175 mL
8	crêpes	8

Preheat oven to 350°F (180°C).

1 Toast shelled hazelnuts 12 to 15 minutes in oven or until nicely browned. Shake pan occasionally to brown evenly. Remove nuts from oven and let cool.

2 Increase oven temperature to 425°F (220°C).

3 Place nuts in food processor and blend about 1 minute. Set aside.

4 Place butter and ½ cup (125 mL) sugar in small bowl. Cream together. Add ground nuts and mix well.

5 Spread hazelnut butter over each crêpe. Fold in four and place crêpes on ovenproof platter. Top with remaining sugar.

6 Cook 2 to 3 minutes in oven. Be careful not to burn crêpes. Serve with an apricot coulis, if desired.

Raspberry Crêpes with Sabayon
(6 servings)

SABAYON:

3	large egg yolks	3
¼ cup	superfine sugar	50 mL
½ cup	white wine (not too dry)	125 mL
1 tsp	grated orange zest	5 mL

1 Place all ingredients in double boiler set over low heat. Whisk until mixture becomes thick.

CRÊPES:

2 tbsp	butter	30 mL
2 tbsp	superfine sugar	30 mL
2 cups	fresh raspberries, cleaned	500 mL
2 tbsp	orange liqueur	30 mL
12	dessert crêpes	12

1 Heat butter in frying pan over medium heat. Add sugar and cook 2 minutes, stirring constantly with fork.

2 Add raspberries and mix well. Continue cooking 2 minutes. Pour in liqueur and flambé.

3 Spread mixture over crêpes, roll and place on ovenproof platter. Broil 2 minutes in oven, then serve with sabayon.

Strawberry and Cream Cheese Crêpes
(4 servings)

¾ lb	fresh strawberries, cleaned, hulled and sliced	350 g
⅓ cup	superfine sugar	75 mL
3 oz	soft cream cheese	90 g
1 tbsp	Cointreau (orange liqueur)	15 mL
8	crêpes	8
	extra superfine sugar	

1 Place strawberries and sugar in saucepan. Cook 12 minutes over low heat or until mixture becomes thick. Transfer to bowl and let cool.

2 Place cream cheese in small bowl and pour in liqueur. Whisk until smooth and light.

3 Spread small amount of cheese over each crêpe. Top with berry mixture, roll and place on oven-proof platter. Sprinkle with more sugar and broil 2 minutes in oven. Serve.

Crêpes with Strawberries and Honey
(4 servings)

⅓ cup	softened butter	75 mL
¼ cup	honey	50 mL
8	dessert crêpes	8
24	fresh strawberries, cleaned, hulled and sliced	24
1 tbsp	superfine sugar	15 mL

1 Mix butter and honey together; spread over crêpes.

2 Top crêpes with sliced strawberries and roll. Place crêpes on ovenproof platter and sprinkle with sugar.

3 Broil in oven 2 minutes on each side or until lightly browned. Serve hot.

Crêpes Normandy
(4 to 6 servings)

4 tbsp	butter	60 mL
6	apples, cored, peeled and sliced	6
2 tbsp	brown sugar	30 mL
3 tbsp	Calvados brandy	45 mL
8 – 12	crêpes	8 – 12
	pinch of cinnamon	
	superfine sugar	

1 Heat butter in frying pan over medium heat. Add apples and brown sugar. Cook 2 minutes. Reduce heat to low, cover and cook another 4 minutes.

2 Remove cover. Mix in brandy and cinnamon; cook 2 minutes.

3 Divide apples among crêpes and roll. Place on ovenproof platter and sprinkle with superfine sugar. Broil 3 minutes in oven. Serve.

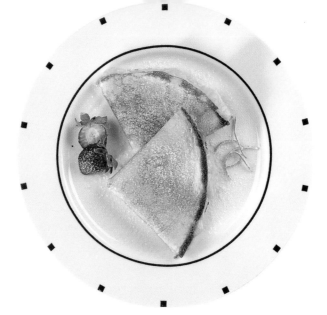

Orange Brunch Crêpes
(8 to 12 servings)

2 cups	all-purpose flour	500 mL
½ cup	granulated sugar	125 mL
5	eggs, beaten	5
1½ cups	milk	375 mL
3 tbsp	melted butter	45 mL
½ cup	softened butter	125 mL
¾ cup	confectioners' sugar	175 mL
	pinch of salt	
	grated zest of 2 oranges	
	grated zest of 1 lemon	
	superfine sugar	

1 Sift flour, salt and granulated sugar into bowl. Add eggs and mix well with wooden spoon. Pour in milk and whisk to incorporate. Mix in melted butter.

2 Pass batter through sieve into clean bowl. Mix in zest of 1 orange and 1 lemon. Cover with plastic wrap touching surface and refrigerate 1 hour.

3 Bring batter to room temperature and make crêpes.

4 Mix softened butter with confectioners' sugar and remaining orange zest.

5 Spread orange butter over each crêpe. Fold in four and place on ovenproof platter. Sprinkle with superfine sugar. Broil 3 minutes in oven until lightly browned. Serve at once.

Crêpes Surprise
(6 servings)

2 tbsp	butter	30 mL
4	pears, peeled, cored and diced	4
2 tbsp	granulated sugar	30 mL
2 tbsp	orange liqueur	30 mL
	dessert crêpe batter	

1 Heat butter in frying pan over medium heat. Add pears and sugar; cook 2 minutes.

2 Pour in liqueur and continue cooking 2 minutes. Turn off heat under pan.

3 Following technique for making crêpes (page 33), pour small amount of batter into buttered, hot crêpe pan. Cook for about 1 minute or until edges start to brown.

4 Place small amount of pears in middle of cooking crêpe. Add more crêpe batter to cover pears and continue cooking 30 seconds.

5 Flip stuffed crêpe over and cook 1 minute. Fold in two and serve. Repeat procedure for remaining batter.

Crêpes Bretonnes
(4 servings)

½ cup	buckwheat flour	125 mL
½ cup	all-purpose flour	125 mL
½ tsp	salt	2 mL
3	large eggs	3
1 cup	milk	250 mL
4 tbsp	melted butter	60 mL
	strawberry or raspberry jam	
	granulated sugar	

1 Sift both flours and salt into bowl. Add eggs and mix with wooden spoon. Pour in milk and whisk to incorporate. Mix in butter.

2 Pass batter through sieve into clean bowl. Cover with plastic wrap touching surface and refrigerate 1 hour.

3 Bring batter to room temperature and make crêpes.

4 Spread jam over crêpes. Fold in four and place on ovenproof platter. Sprinkle with sugar and broil 1 minute in oven. Turn crêpes over, broil another minute and serve.

Decadent Chocolate Crêpes with Ice Cream
(4 servings)

¼ lb	sweet baking chocolate	125 g
½ cup	water	125 mL
2 tbsp	Cointreau (orange liqueur)	30 mL
8	crêpes	8
1⅔ cup	vanilla ice cream	400 mL
	pinch of salt	

1 Place chocolate, water and salt in double boiler. Melt over very low heat until smooth and glossy. Stir constantly! Remove from heat and mix in liqueur.

2 Spoon about ¼ cup (50 mL) of vanilla ice cream on each crêpe. Roll and place on ovenproof platter. Broil 2 minutes in oven.

3 Drizzle chocolate sauce over crêpes and serve immediately.

Cream-Stuffed Crêpes with Pears
(6 to 8 servings)

4	pears, cored, peeled and sliced	4
3 tbsp	superfine sugar	45 mL
½	recipe Dessert Cream Filling (see page 94)	½
12	crêpes	12
¼ cup	toasted slivered almonds	50 mL
	sugar	

1 Place pears and superfine sugar in saucepan. Cook 10 minutes over medium heat. Remove pan from heat and let cool.

2 Spread 2 tbsp (30 mL) of dessert cream filling over each crêpe. Add some of pears and fold in four. Place crêpes on ovenproof platter and sprinkle with sugar.

3 Broil 3 minutes in oven. Garnish servings with toasted almonds. Serve with a raspberry coulis, if desired.

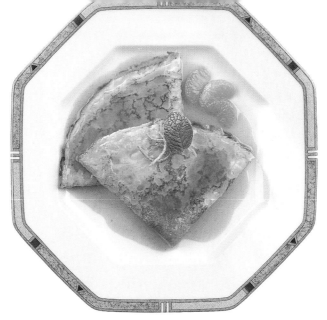

Crêpes Suzette with Curaçao
(4 servings)

8	thin dessert crêpes	8
4 tbsp	unsalted butter	60 mL
4 tbsp	superfine sugar	60 mL
4 tbsp	Curaçao (orange liqueur)	60 mL
	juice of 3 tangerines	

1 Fold crêpes in four and set aside.

2 Place butter and sugar in chafing dish or large frying pan. Melt over medium heat, stirring constantly with fork.

3 When mixture becomes golden brown, add tangerine juice. Mix quickly until sauce becomes smooth.

4 Place crêpes in sauce and cook 30 seconds. Turn crêpes over and pour in liqueur. Flambé and serve.

Basic White Sauce
(yield: 1¾ cups (450 mL))

3 tbsp	butter	45 mL
3 tbsp	all-purpose flour	45 mL
2 cups	milk, heated	500 mL
	salt and white pepper	
	pinch of ground cloves	
	ground nutmeg to taste	

1 Heat butter in saucepan over medium heat. Sprinkle in flour and mix very well. Cook 1 minute over low heat.

2 Add milk, 1 cup (250 mL) at a time, whisking between additions. Add all seasonings and mix again.

3 Cook sauce 12 minutes over low heat, stirring often during cooking.

4 Use immediately or cover with plastic wrap, touching surface. Sauce will keep up to 2 days in refrigerator.

Note: For **Thick White Sauce**, use 1½ cups (375 mL) milk instead of 2 cups (500 mL).

Mornay Sauce
(4 to 6 servings)

4 tbsp	butter	60 mL
4 tbsp	flour	60 mL
2 cups	milk, heated	500 mL
1	small onion, peeled	1
1	clove	1
⅓ cup	grated Gruyère cheese	75 mL
3 tbsp	grated Parmesan cheese	45 mL
	salt and white pepper	
	pinch of nutmeg	

1 Heat butter in saucepan over medium heat. Sprinkle in flour, mix well and cook 1 minute over low heat.

2 Incorporate milk and season with salt, pepper and nutmeg. Stud onion with clove and add to sauce.

3 Bring to boil and simmer 12 minutes over low heat. Stir frequently with whisk.

4 Remove studded onion. Pass sauce through sieve into clean saucepan. Stir in both cheeses and simmer 2 minutes.

Egg Sauce
(4 to 6 servings)

3 tbsp	butter	45 mL
3 tbsp	flour	45 mL
2 cups	milk, heated	500 mL
2	egg yolks, lightly beaten	2
2	egg whites, beaten stiff	2
½ cup	grated sharp cheese of your choice	125 mL
	salt and pepper	
	pinch of paprika	

1 Heat butter in saucepan over medium heat. Sprinkle in flour and mix well. Cook 1 minute.

2 Pour in milk and mix rapidly with whisk until smooth. Season with salt, pepper and paprika. Cook sauce 12 minutes over medium-low heat, stirring frequently.

3 Mix in egg yolks and remove pan from heat.

4 Fold in egg whites and cheese. Correct seasoning.

Note: Use this sauce with a variety of fillings for crêpes.

Pastry Cream

2 cups	milk	500 mL
1 tsp	pure vanilla	5 mL
1	large egg	1
2	large egg yolks	2
½ cup	granulated sugar	125 mL
½ cup	all-purpose flour	125 mL
4 tbsp	unsalted butter	60 mL
3 tbsp	Kirsch brandy	45 mL

1 Bring milk and vanilla to boiling point in saucepan over medium heat. As soon as liquid starts to bubble, remove pan from heat and set aside.

2 Place all eggs in bowl. Using electric hand mixer, beat until foamy. Add sugar and continue beating until mixture becomes pale yellow in color.

3 Add flour and beat just long enough to incorporate.

4 Incorporate most of hot milk while beating constantly. Add remaining milk, mix well, and pour contents of bowl into saucepan.

5 Bring cream to boil over medium heat, stirring constantly. Cook 1 minute longer, then remove pan from heat.

6 Stir in butter until melted, then transfer cream to clean bowl. Mix in brandy and cover with plastic wrap touching surface. Let cool before refrigerating.

Note: If you prefer a lighter cream, fold in 1 or 2 stiff egg whites at the end of cooking when the cream is still hot.

Place all eggs in bowl. Using electric hand mixer, beat until foamy.

Add sugar and continue beating until mixture becomes pale yellow in color.

Add flour and beat just long enough to incorporate.

Incorporate hot milk while beating constantly.

Bring cream to boil over medium heat, stirring constantly. Cook 1 minute longer, then remove pan from heat. Stir in butter until melted, then transfer cream to clean bowl.

Dessert Cream Filling

¾ cup	superfine sugar	175 mL
1	large egg	1
2	large egg yolks	2
5 tbsp	flour	75 mL
1½ cups	milk, heated	375 mL
2 oz	Kirsch brandy	60 mL

1 Place sugar, whole egg and egg yolks in bowl. Using electric hand mixer, beat 7 minutes.

2 Stir in flour and beat 30 seconds. Incorporate hot milk and mix until cream becomes smooth.

3 Transfer contents of bowl to saucepan. Cook over low heat until sauce becomes thick, about 5 to 6 minutes. Stir constantly.

4 Pour sauce into clean bowl and stir in brandy. Cover with plastic wrap and let cool to room temperature.

5 Cream filling will keep up to 2 days in refrigerator.

Basic Chocolate Sauce

1 cup	confectioners' sugar	250 mL
2 oz	bitter baking chocolate	60 g
1 tsp	pure vanilla	5 mL
3 tbsp	light cream	45 mL
1	egg yolk	1

1 Place confectioners' sugar, chocolate, vanilla and cream in stainless steel bowl. Set bowl over saucepan half-filled with hot water.

2 Melt over low heat.

3 Remove bowl from saucepan and whisk. Add egg yolk and whisk to incorporate.

4 Cover with plastic wrap and keep warm until ready to serve. Use this sauce the same day it is made.

INDEX